DATE DUE

CAREER SKILLS LIBRARY

COMMUNICATION
SKILLS

THE CAREER SKILLS LIBRARY

Communication Skills
By Richard Worth

Information Management
By Joseph Mackall

Leadership Skills
By Diane E. Rossiter

Learning the Ropes
By Sharon Naylor

Organization Skills
By Richard Worth

Problem-Solving
By Dandi Daley Mackall

Self-Development
By Dandi Daley Mackall

Teamwork Skills
By Dandi Daley Mackall

COMMUNICATION
S K I L L S.

by Richard Worth

A New England Publishing Associates Book

Copyright ©1998 by Ferguson Publishing Company, Chicago, Illinois

Printed in the United States of America
U-8

Library of Congress Cataloging-in-Publication Data

Worth, Richard.
    Communication skills / by Richard Worth.
       p. cm.
    Includes bibliographical references and index.
    Summary: Discusses communication skills needed in the workplace, including writing concise reports, public speaking, and communicating in meetings and other company settings.
    ISBN 0-89434-209-6
    1. Business communication. 2. Commercial correspondence. 3. Public speaking. 4. Listening. [1. Business communication.] I. Title
    HF5718.W67   1998
    55.17—dc21   97-26628
                                       CIP
                                       AC

4

CONTENTS

INTRODUCTION

Communication fills much of our lives. We sit in school and listen to teachers. We read books and magazines. We talk to friends, watch television, communicate over the Internet.

The workplace is no different. Experts tell us that 70% to 80% of our working time is spent in some kind of communication. We are reading and writing memos, listening to our coworkers, and having one-to-one conversations with our supervisors.

Communication involves at least two people: the *sender* and the *receiver.* In this book, we'll look at four types of communication between senders and receivers: writing, speaking, listening, and conducting meetings. Each one is important to your success in the workplace.

For example, a poorly written application letter can prevent you from being hired for a job. On the other hand, the ability to write effectively and make clear presentations can make the difference between being promoted or being left behind. As Ken Matejka and Diane Ramos explain in their book *Hook 'em,* "You need effective, persuasive communication skills for career advancement."

A communication skill that's often overlooked is listening. Yet recent surveys tell us that we spend 45% of our time listening. Do we listen carefully to what people are telling us? According to one study, we hear only one quarter of what's being said. The rest of the time we're daydreaming or just tuned out.

A communication skill that's often overlooked is listening.

How We Spend Our Communication Time

9%	writing
16%	reading
30%	talking
45%	listening

One sales manager in a printing company tells the story of needing a job rushed through in 24 hours so his best customer could have it on time. He gave careful instructions to the production supervisor. But before he could finish, the supervisor already had stopped listening. He assumed that the customer wanted the job three days later, which was the usual deadline for most of these projects. When the sales manager went to pick up the job the next day, it wasn't ready. As a result, he almost lost the customer. Unfortunately, stories like this are common in many organizations.

Listening, writing, and speaking are all skills we use in meetings. Today, meetings are a common method for making decisions. More and more work is done by teams of people who come from different areas of a company. They accomplish many of their tasks in team meetings. In these situations, we must be able to speak and write clearly so others can understand us and listen carefully to what they say. Sadly, many hours are wasted in meetings because of poor communication. A study by one university estimated that $37 billion is lost annually through unproductive meetings.

Whether you're writing, listening, speaking, or attending meetings, communication skills are critical to your success in the workplace. In this book, we'll look at some of the skills that will enable your communications to be more successful. These include:

Listening, writing and speaking are all skills we use in meetings.

▶ Understand the purpose of a communication.

▶ Analyze the audience.

▶ Communicate with your words as well as your body language.

▶ Give each communication greater impact.

CHAPTER ONE
WRITE FOR YOUR READERS
(Or Write With A Purpose)

Jill's boss asked her to write a memo on a school-to-work program. The company where Jill worked was a leader in the computer software field. A school-to-work program would give young people in school a chance to be employed part-time and learn the software business. If their work was good, the company might hire them for full-time jobs after they graduated.

"Keep the memo short," Jill's boss told her. "And stick to the point."

Jill was supposed to explain the type of program her company should start. She sat down at her computer and began to write. On the first page, she talked about her own experience in a school-to-work program. Then she described what two of her friends had done in their programs. They had worked part-time in other companies. Next she wrote about several school-to-work programs described in magazines. Five pages later, she finally signed her name.

"Well, I think the information my boss wants is in here somewhere," she said to herself. Then she submitted the memo.

Jill's boss was a very busy person. He received more than 50 memos each day. He didn't have time to read every memo completely. A memo writer had to get to the point quickly. Otherwise, Jill's boss would read no further. He read the first paragraph of Jill's memo. Then he scanned the second paragraph.

"What's the point of this memo?" he asked himself. He threw up his hands in frustration. Then he threw the memo into the wastebasket.

INFORMATION OVERLOAD

In the workplace, information seems to come from all directions. Each day managers are expected to read memos, letters, and reports. They arrive by e-mail, over the fax machine and by overnight delivery. With so much information coming in, managers don't have time to read all of it. Often they will stop reading a memo if it doesn't capture their interest very quickly.

How can you make sure that your memo will be read? How can you be certain that what you have written will be remembered by your boss? You must have a clear purpose and state that purpose as quickly as possible. This was something that Jill neglected to do in her memo. It's also essential that you know your reader and give him the information he wants. Jill's boss wanted a concise memo that explained the type of school-to-work program the company should adopt. Instead Jill gave him a rambling, five-page report that didn't tell him what he wanted to know. As a result, it ended up in the wastebasket.

You must have a clear purpose and state that purpose as quickly as possible.

F A C T O I D :

A young manager who runs one of America's leading mutual funds says that she receives over 200 faxes daily.

DEFINE YOUR PURPOSE

Many people just sit down and begin writing and hope for the best. Sometimes, they are lucky. Most of the time they produce something that is poorly written and confusing. Before you begin writing, state your purpose and how you propose to carry it out. These can be stated briefly in one or two *summary sentences.* These sentences sum up the purpose of your writing.

If you cannot express in a sentence or two what you intend to get across, then it is not focused well enough.

— Charles Osgood
TV Commentator

Suppose you want your school to sponsor a class trip. You decide to write a letter to the principal about it. Here are your summary sentences:

My letter is designed to persuade the principal to sponsor the trip. The letter will present three reasons why the trip would be valuable for students.

The purpose of some writing is to *persuade.* We use this type of writing at school and on the job. Jan believed that her office needed more computers. Without them, she and her co-workers simply couldn't keep up with the volume of work. Jan wrote a memo to her boss to persuade him to purchase additional computers. She pointed out that everyone would get more work done if the computers were purchased. She also found a company that sold computers at a very low price. These arguments convinced her boss to buy them.

The purpose of some writing is to *explain.* One student worked part-time at a pet store that sold fish. She had to write a memo for new employees on how to feed each type of fish. Here are her summary sentences:

My memo explains the feeding times for each fish. It also explains the type of food and quantity of food that each fish should receive.

Some writing is primarily designed to *describe.* Robert's supervisor sent him to a conference and wanted him to write a memo describing what happened there. Robert knew his supervisor didn't want to know everything that occurred, only the most important things. Here is his summary sentence:

I will describe the three significant things I learned at the conference that might help our department.

DOS AND DON'TS
OF SUMMARY SENTENCES

▶ Do write the summary sentences before doing anything else.

▶ Do keep your sentences short.

▶ Don't exceed one or two sentences for each writing project.

▶ Don't include any information in your paper that doesn't relate to the summary sentences.

▶ Do specify whether the purpose of your writing is to persuade, explain, or describe.

15

FACTOID:

An estimated 85% of our success in business is determined by our communication skills.

EXERCISE

Write one or two summary sentences for a short paper:

1. explaining how to be a successful student.

2. persuading an employer to hire you for a part-time job.

3. describing what happened at an important meeting you attended as part of an extracurricular activity.

WRITING FOR YOUR READER

Some people keep diaries or journals. This type of writing is meant only for themselves. However, most writing is meant to be read by somebody else. Thus, it's important for you to know as much as possible about your readers. This information will help you decide what to say and how to say it.

Questions to Ask About Your Readers

▶ Who are they?

▶ What do they need to know?

▶ What is their attitude?

▶ Why should they care?

A human resources manager at a manufacturing company explains that some new employees often don't understand the "politics" of the organization. Suppose they think a supervisor is treating them unfairly. They're apt to fire off a memo telling him about it. Unfortunately, they don't last very long in the organization. You may be able to complain about unfair treatment to your co-workers, but new employees are not expected to criticize their boss.

Before you send off a memo or a letter, it is very important to understand your readers. What can you say? What can't you say? What do they expect from you?

It is very important to understand your readers.

Some supervisors only are interested in facts and figures. Suppose you are proposing a new project. They only want to know how it will benefit the organization, how much it will cost, and how you will carry it out. If this is what your supervisor expects, then give it to her.

Other supervisors also are interested in learning about the steps you followed in conceptualizing the project. They want to know where you gathered your information and what other companies have undertaken similar projects. They also may be interested in finding out about alternative approaches to executing the project that you considered but later rejected. These supervisors are more process and detail oriented. If this is the type of supervisor that you work for, then be sure to give him the information he wants. Otherwise, your project proposal may not be approved.

Dos and Don'ts
OF WRITING FOR YOUR READER

▶ Do remember that all communication is written for a reader.

▶ Do analyze your readers before you begin writing.

▶ Don't leave out any important information that the reader needs to know.

▶ Don't forget that the readers' attitudes will influence how they respond to your writing.

▶ Do make your writing appeal to what the reader cares most about.

Another important question to ask yourself when you write is: What information does the reader need to know? Suppose you are trying to transfer to another department in your company. You begin your letter this way:

I am applying for the position posted by your department.

Unfortunately the department has posted more than one position. If you don't indicate which position you want, the reader will not be able to tell whether you have the proper qualifications. Therefore, you probably will not get the job.

Never assume. One of the biggest mistakes some writers make is to assume their readers have knowledge that they do not have. Suppose you are explaining a complicated procedure on a computer. Do not assume that the reader already understands some of the steps. Be sure to describe everything carefully.

If you are trying to persuade readers to do something, it helps to understand their attitude. Are they likely to support you? Are they likely to oppose you? Are they neutral? This information helps you decide how persuasive you must be.

PROPOSAL TO THE PRINCIPAL

A group of students wanted to persuade their principal to support a new project. They wanted to have time off for a half day of community service each week. The principal was in favor of community service. She was opposed to letting students take time away from class to do these projects.

The students explained that the community projects would support what they were learning in school. They would improve their communication skills by writing reports about the projects. Some of the projects required them to analyze and summarize data. This work improved their math skills. The students realized that the principal was worried that they might lose learning time. They knew their reader, so they designed arguments that would persuade her. Eventually she agreed to try out one community service project to see how it worked.

The final important question you must ask yourself when you write is: What do my readers care about? By mentioning something they care about, you can hook their attention. You also can persuade them to do what you want. Earlier we mentioned a supervisor who cared only about facts and figures. By writing about what she cared about, you could persuade her to adopt your project. Suppose you wanted to con-

(Courtesy: Haddam-Killingworth High School)

How would you write a bulletin board notice that would hook your reader's attention?

vince other students to join your club. You decide to put a notice up on the bulletin board about an upcoming club meeting. How would you begin the notice in order to hook the reader's attention? By mentioning something that they might care about. Perhaps joining the club will enable them to have fun with friends, or learn a new skill, or make money. Each of these might persuade them to join your club.

> **EXERCISE**
>
> Write a notice for a club to persuade other students to join it.

THE 4 Cs OF SUCCESSFUL WRITING

All good writing starts by defining your purpose and knowing your reader. But that's only a beginning. There are four other elements that you should also keep in mind. They are known as the 4 Cs:

- ► 1. Concise
- ► 2. Compelling
- ► 3. Clear
- ► 4. Correct

BE CONCISE
The Job Application Letter.

Job application letters (also called cover letters) usually accompany resumes. Both the letter and resume are sent into an employer when you are applying for a job. The resume and application letter discuss your qualifications for a job. The letter mentions them briefly. The resume goes into more detail.

"I had one student," explains career counselor Rozanne Burt, "who was having a difficult time writ-

(V. Harlow/Electrical Associates)

Employers sometimes receive a hundred or more resumes when they advertise an opening. To get in the door for an interview, you must write a persuasive cover letter that shows you're an ideal candidate.

ing a job application letter. I told him to keep the letter to a page or less and only highlight his most important accomplishments. But he couldn't or wouldn't be selective. Instead he wanted to include everything. He ended up with a letter that ran over a page and a half in tiny, nine-point type. Needless to say, the employer was not impressed and he didn't get the job."

With all the information that employers have to read today, the last thing they want is something that's long-winded. It's essential to be concise. Human resources director Debby Berggren receives a lot of application letters from people looking for jobs. And she says that many people have trouble "getting to the point."

If you want to write a concise application letter, or any other type of letter, it's important to understand the purpose of the letter before you begin writing. If you were to compose your summary sentences for an application letter, they might sound like this: *My letter persuades an employer to interview me. It includes several of my outstanding accomplishments to convince an employer that I am right for the job.*

The purpose of a cover letter is to persuade.

The purpose of a cover letter is to persuade—to persuade an employer to interview you for a job. The next step is to know your reader. What will the reader find most persuasive? You need to select the skills and experience that you possess which will convince the reader to interview you. As Burt explains: "You can't tell them everything about you, so you have to stick to a few things that are linked to what the employer values, and you have to nail down what you want them to know early in the letter."

One of the most effective methods of writing is called the *pyramid style.* You put the most important information at the top of the pyramid, the beginning of the letter. And you present it as simply and concisely as possible. You follow this with the second most important point, the third, the fourth, and so forth. This is the same style that newspaper reporters have used for years to write news articles.

THE PYRAMID STYLE OF WRITING

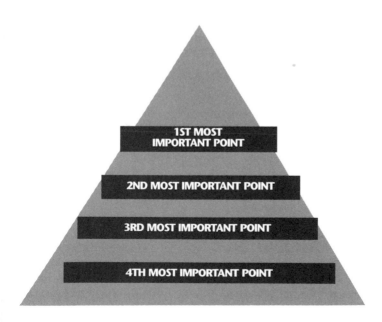

1ST MOST IMPORTANT POINT

2ND MOST IMPORTANT POINT

3RD MOST IMPORTANT POINT

4TH MOST IMPORTANT POINT

In a job application letter, the most important information to mention is the position for which you are applying. Otherwise, the reader won't know why you are writing. This information goes in the first paragraph. The second paragraph should describe the one or two skills or work experiences that make you most qualified for the job.

This is where you hook the reader's attention by telling her something she cares about and persuading her to consider you for the position. A third paragraph might mention several additional, but less important qualifications you possess. Finally, you should conclude the letter by asking for an interview.

EXERCISE

Write a job application letter. Select a position for which you are qualified based on your work experience and skills.

BE COMPELLING
The Resume.

"Employers may get as many as 300 resumes for one job," explains career counselor John Jarvis. "So they have to find a way to narrow them down. Some

MARIA'S LETTER

January 1, 2000
Ms. Julie Rogers
All-Occasion Clothing Store
10 Prospect Street
Anywhere, USA 09999-0999

Dear Ms. Rogers,

I am applying for the position of assistant manager, which you recently advertised in the *Evening Times*.

During the past three years, I have worked part-time as a sales associate at Calloway and Company, the largest department store in the area. I was twice voted Employee of the Month. I received this award in recognition of my service to customers. Calloway and Company also promoted me to assistant manager of my department.

I am graduating in June with an associate's degree in retailing. My grade point average has been 3.6, and I have taken courses in marketing and sales as well as accounting.

I look forward to speaking with you in the near future and discussing what I can contribute to your organization.

Sincerely,

Maria Gonzales

employers tell me that they put the one-page resumes in one pile, and the two-page resumes go in the trash."

Like the application or cover letter, the resume persuades an employer to hire you. As Jarvis points out, many employers like a concise resume. Anything over a page is too long. The resume must also be compelling to hook an employer's interest. How do you make it compelling?

Many employers like a concise resume.

Once again, you must start with a clear purpose. This is usually called your "job objective." The job objective goes near the top of a resume, so the employer will know immediately what type of job you're seeking.

Let's look at Maria's resume, which she developed to accompany her application letter.

The most compelling type of writing has a clear purpose. Your readers know immediately why you are writing. In the case of a resume, they know immediately what job you want. Compelling writing is also designed to appeal to your readers. How do you accomplish this on a resume?

Make the resume visually interesting.

One way is to make the resume visually interesting. This means using different kinds of type. For example, Maria puts her headings in boldface type. She also uses bullets to set off key points. White space

MARIA'S RESUME

MARIA GONZALES
328 Cedar Street
Anywhere, USA 09999-9990
(999) 562-3147

Job Objective   To obtain a position as an assistant manager in a retail store.

Experience

1994-Present   Calloway and Company

• Worked as sales associate in women's casual clothing
• Advanced to Assistant Department Manager
• Won Employee of the Month Award three times
• Successfully completed sales training program

1992-1994   Downtown CDS and Tapes

• Part-time stock clerk
• Trained other clerks

Education

Associate's Degree in Retailing
Central Community College
GPA: 3.6
Courses: Marketing, Sales, Accounting, Economics

Honors Graduate, Longwood High School
Vice President of Senior Class
Member of soccer and tennis teams

References   Available upon request.

also is important. Don't try to cram too much information on a resume. The resume will look too crowded. Instead, keep it simple.

_____

The resume doesn't get you the job. It gets you the interview. Don't overwhelm them with the resume.

—John Jarvis
Career Counselor

Remember also to use dynamic words to describe your accomplishments. For example, always try to use verbs in the active voice, not the passive voice. "I *was given* the Employee of the Month Award," uses a passive verb, which sounds weak. Maria presents this information in a stronger way by writing: "Won Employee of the Month Award." Instead of saying "I *was appointed* Assistant Department Manager," Maria says, "*Advanced* to Assistant Department Manager." Finally, instead of writing "*I was asked to train* other clerks," Maria writes "*Trained* other clerks."

Descriptive words also make your writing more compelling. And these words can be especially powerful on a resume. Don't exaggerate what you have accomplished but use descriptive words to bring it to life. Instead of saying, "completed a training course,"

Maria writes, "*Successfully* completed sales training program." If you are a "*fully* experienced" stock clerk, say so. If you have "*extensive* knowledge" of computers, include that information as well. These simple descriptive words stand out on the page and attract the reader's attention.

Chris Hanson is applying for a part-time job after school. He wants to be an animal handler or kennel worker. Chris has worked part-time for three years at the local Audubon Society. He has valuable experi-

Volunteering at a maritime aquarium will give this young man valuable work experience to bolster his resume.

ence caring for sick and injured animals. He also trained other volunteers to care for the animals. Before this, Chris volunteered at a local nature center. He completed a training course in how to conduct tours of the center. Every Saturday, he conducted tours for up to fifty adults and children. Currently, Chris is attending high school where he writes for the newspaper and maintains a 3.2 GPA.

EXERCISE

1. Use the information about Chris to develop a brief resume that he can use to find a job.

2. Write a resume for yourself. It should reflect the application letter that you wrote in the preceding exercise.

BE CLEAR
Memos and Reports.

Good writing is simple and clear. You should leave no doubt in the minds of your readers what you are trying to say to them. Unfortunately, some people seem to forget this principle when they write.

A task force from the National Council of Teachers of English and the International Reading Association recently tried to develop national standards on how to write English. They came up with 12 basic rules. Rule number 5 states "Students employ a wide range of strategies as they write and use different writing process elements appropriately to communicate with different audiences for a variety of purposes." What is a process element? What does the panel mean by "communicate with different audiences for a variety of purposes?" These terms are so vague that no one could be sure. The *New York Times* wrote that the rules were written in "a tongue barely recognizable as English." And they were written by English teachers!

American executives...rate a third of all the business material they have to read as "unclear, poorly written, or confusing."

—Kenneth Roman and Joel Raphaelson in *Writing That Works*

Some writers seem to think that you need big, fancy-sounding words to lend importance to a subject. Too often, these words make the subject far more complicated than it needs to be. Even worse, your readers may not understand what you mean.

Jason works in an office. His supervisor asked him to write a brief memo and post it in the coffee room. Here's what Jason wrote:

TO: All Employees

FM: Supervisor

SUBJ: Snacks

The ongoing procedure of making available a variety of snacks on a pre-payment basis is undergoing reconsideration. In the event that employees who appropriate these food items without leaving the proper remuneration do not terminate these activities, the snacks will be eliminated in the future.

Jason used a lot of long, high-sounding words because he was trying to sound important. After all, he had been asked to write this memo by his supervisor. But the meaning of what Jason was saying was not very clear. He really could have written it very simply: "We will no longer have snacks available if employees don't pay for them."

In his book, *Writing That Works*, Richard Anderson advises, "Use words that are easy to pronounce and everyone can understand. Long and unfamiliar words slow readers down, and readers who slow down often

34

stop." You don't want your readers to stop reading, or they will lose the message that you are trying to communicate.

One sure way to stop readers cold in their tracks is to write long, involved sentences that are difficult to follow. Cheryl was asked by her supervisor to write a brief report on the training program she attended at the restaurant where she worked. She began the report this way:

> The training program, whose interesting classes, excellent instruction, and extensive hands-on experience, afforded me a unique glimpse at different types of jobs in our organization, and it, right from the start of the program and the very first class which I attended more than two weeks ago, gave me the chance to meet some of the people with whom I will be working in the future, since they were in my training classes.

One sure way to stop readers cold in their tracks is to write long, involved sentences that are difficult to follow.

This sentence is 73 words long. If you try to read it aloud, it will leave you completely out of breath. Since there are several important ideas in the sentence—why the training program was effective, what Cheryl learned and whom she met—they could easily be presented as separate sentences.

Cheryl's sentence also has other problems. Sentences are easy to understand when the subjects and verbs are close together: "She writes a report." But Cheryl separates her subjects and verbs by long clauses. In the first part of the sentence, the subject "program" is separated from the verb "afforded." In the second part of the sentence the subject "it" also is separated by a long clause from the verb "gave." This makes her writing hard to follow. Cheryl also uses far more words than she needs to communicate her ideas. The sentence might be rewritten this way:

The training program featured interesting classes, excellent instruction, and extensive hands-on experience. It taught me about many types of jobs. I also had a chance to meet some of the people who will be working with me.

In business writing, a good rule of thumb is to keep the sentences as easy to understand as possible. If you have two important ideas to present, use two separate sentences. And eliminate all unnecessary words.

EXERCISE

Re-write the following sentences to make them clearer and simpler.

1. Greenway Tree Farms, because of the strong price for Christmas trees, a larger demand for trees expected during the holiday season and the improving economy in the eastern and southern regions of the country, will probably experience continued growth in the fourth quarter.

2. Our sales representatives, since they may be new employees in our firm and are not always informed about the products which they are supposed to be describing to our customers, may sound embarrassed and confused and, even worse, cause confusion in the minds of the customers.

BE CORRECT

Career counselor John Jarvis explains what one employer was looking for in the position of administrative assistant. "He emphasized communication skills," Jarvis said. "He didn't want to waste time proofing the administrative assistant's work. He wanted to dictate the letter, and expected his assistant to punctuate it correctly and use proper spelling and capitalization."

The workplace is different from school. In your classes Bs and Cs may be acceptable. Your teachers will allow you to make a few mistakes. On the job, mistakes detract from the impact of your writing. A misspelled word, a comma in the wrong place, a period where there should be a question mark—all of these mistakes distract the reader from what you're trying to say. They tell the reader that your writing is sloppy. Furthermore, it implies that if your writing is sloppy, perhaps your thinking is sloppy, as well.

Now that most writers use a computer, they rely on spell-check to catch those misspelled words. But spell-check can take you only so far. It will correct misspellings. However, it will not tell you if you're using the wrong word in a specific situation. One computer consulting firm submitted a proposal to a large landscaping company to upgrade their computer system. The proposal was designed to be a "turnkey" operation, which meant that all the hardware and software would be installed. And the system would be ready to use. Instead of "turnkey," the proposal said "turkey" operation. Spell-check

(V. Harlow/Russell Library)

Using a computer spell-checker is a good idea. But remember a spell-checker won't catch the difference between "to", "two" and "too".

did not catch this mistake because "turkey" is a word, just like "turnkey." No one had bothered to proofread the proposal adequately.

Sometimes we may use the wrong word in a situation. The table on the next page provides a list of sound-alike and look-alike words that give many writers trouble. Of course, there are others, too. If you have a question about which word to use in a specific sentence, look up the word in a dictionary.

SOUND ALIKE AND LOOK ALIKE WORDS

Accept	receive	*Except*	exclude
Affect	influence (verb)	*Effect*	result (noun), bring about
Complement	something that completes	*Compliment*	praise
Desert	dry landscape	*Dessert*	last course of a meal
Eminent	famous	*Imminent*	about to happen
Foreword	introduction to a book	*Forward*	ahead; toward the front
Illusion	a false impression	*Allusion*	reference to something else
Precede	come before	*Proceed*	go forward
Principal	person who runs a school	*Principle*	a truth or value
Stationary	in a fixed position	*Stationery*	writing paper
Tacked	to add on or attach	*Tact*	sensitivity to another's feelings
Tic	an involuntary spasm; twitching	*Tick*	the sound of a clock; a tiny insect
Toe	appendages of the foot	*Tow*	the act of pulling
Trade-in	(noun) an exchange	*Trade in*	(verb) to buy or sell goods
Undo	to reverse	*Undue*	excessive

Whenever you write, it's important to proofread your writing carefully before sending it out to a reader. Here are three proofreading rules that may be helpful to you:

1. Don't proofread on the computer. It's too hard to spot mistakes on a screen. Instead, make a hard copy and proof it at your desk.

2. Don't proofread immediately after you've finished writing. You're too close to the project. And you won't see the mistakes very easily. Instead, put the writing away for a day or two and then proofread it.

3. Proofread three times: once for content, clarity, and conciseness; once, for grammar and punctuation; and once to make sure you've used the right words.

THE PITFALLS OF E-MAIL

Many of the problems that afflict writing are now showing up on electronic mail. E-mail has become an effective way of sending memos and other types of communication that must arrive quickly. "I receive e-mail all the time," reports a freelance artist who designs book covers. "But the mistakes, the misspellings are appalling. No one takes any time to write anything."

41

E-mail is subject to the same rules that govern other types of writing. That is, the writing should be clear and concise. Information should be presented in a compelling manner, with no mistakes in grammar, punctuation, or spelling. The purpose of the communication should be clearly stated, and it should be delivered in a way that appeals to the reader.

In their book, *The Elements of E-Mail Style,* David Angell and Brent Heslop explain that information should be presented in short, coherent units. Readers, they say, are "turned off by large chunks of text." They also urge you to keep your language simple. "If a word confuses your readers and sends them scurrying for the dictionary, it has broken their concentration," Angell and Heslop explain. "Simple and familiar words have power."

FACTOID:

The average person in the United States reads at a fifth-grade level.

Good writing will make you stand out.

IMPROVE YOUR WRITING

Good writing will make you stand out. It will help you excel at school, on the job, and in extracurricular activities. How do you improve your writing?

THE TEN COMMANDMENTS OF GOOD WRITING

1. I realize that all good writing must have a clear purpose.

2. I recognize that less is more—too many words can bore my reader.

3. I understand that the most important information belongs at the beginning of my paper.

4. I avoid all mistakes in grammar, punctuation, and spelling.

5. I think about what my readers want before beginning to write.

6. I make an impact on my readers by making my writing powerful.

7. I don't use complex words when I can use simple ones.

8. I leave out all information that does not relate to my main purpose.

9. I use descriptive words to bring my writing to life.

10. I never assume that my readers know more than they do.

In his book *Persuasive Business Proposals,* Tom Sant explains that "you will do a better job of writing if you know what you're trying to accomplish: the *why* of a document." By writing one or two summary sentences before you begin writing, you can state the "why" very simply.

It's also important to define your audience. Figure out who they are, how much information they need, what their attitude is, and how to make them care about your writing. Finally, get to the point quickly and hook the attention of your readers. The pyramid style of writing will help you accomplish these objectives.

Finally, writing should incorporate the 4 Cs. It should be concise, compelling, clear, and correct.

EXERCISE

1. Find examples of writing from magazines and newspapers that you admire. Notice how they try to excite the reader's interest and present main points. Make a folder of powerful writing and refer to it to help with your own writing.

2. Write the first paragraph of a letter asking people to donate their time or an item to a tag sale. The tag sale is designed to raise money for charity. Make sure the paragraph appeals to the reader and utilizes the 4 Cs of good writing.

2 CHAPTER TWO
DO I *HAVE* TO STAND UP AND SPEAK?

Jim was a head counselor at Camp Sunrise. On Awards Day at the end of the season, he was expected to stand up and speak to the large group of campers and their parents who were attending the ceremony. Jim had prepared his talk and even memorized what he wanted to say. But as he sat on the stage, waiting to be introduced, he became very nervous. He had been dreading this moment for days.

Finally, Jim's name was called. He stood up and walked slowly to the podium. As he moved to center stage, his legs felt wobbly. His palms were sweaty. And there was a big hole right in the pit of his stomach. Jim looked out at all those faces. Suddenly, he wished he could disappear.

"Thank you for coming here today," he began in a tense, high-pitched voice. "It's been a wonderful opportunity to work with so many great campers this summer. Now I'd like to tell you a story about one of them."

(Joe Duffy)

"Do I have to stand up and speak?"

All eyes were on him. Everyone seemed to be waiting for him to begin that story. They waited...and waited...and waited. Jim's mind had suddenly gone blank. He couldn't remember what he wanted to say.

"I knew it yesterday," he thought. "Why can't I remember it now? Why?" It seemed like an hour had passed. But in reality it was only 30 seconds. Panic seized him. Jim knew everyone was staring at him. And he just wanted to get out of there. Finally, he could stand it no longer. Jim turned from the audience and fled off the stage.

THE IMPORTANCE OF PUBLIC SPEAKING

The ability to deliver an effective talk is one of the most valuable skills you can possess. If you want to be a leader in school, public speaking often is essential. As a class officer, head of the student council, or president of a club, you often are called on to stand up and speak to a group. Public speaking also is important in the workplace. As Rozanne Burt explains, "The people who can stand up and give a talk stand out and are set apart from other employees."

Yet most people are afraid of public speaking. In fact, recent polls indicate that they fear it more than death itself.

TOP TEN FEARS AMONG AMERICANS

1. Public speaking	**6.** Sickness
2. Heights	**7.** Death
3. Insects	**8.** Flying
4. Financial trouble	**9.** Loneliness
5. Deep water	**10.** Dogs

Stage fright is not uncommon, even among very good speakers. But they generally don't react the way Jim did. Instead, there are several approaches they use to conquer their fears. These are:

Enlist the Aid of the Audience

Remember, the people in the audience genuinely want you to succeed. They've come to hear you speak. They want to know what you have to say to them. Make eye contact with an individual in the audience who is a friend or acquaintance. As you begin to talk, speak only to that individual. By turning a speech into a one-on-one conversation, it will seem less fearful.

The people in the audience genuinely want you to succeed.

Make Your Stage Fright Work for You

Fear requires a lot of energy. Instead of letting the fear undermine your talk, channel this energy in other directions. Let it flow into your hands and arms. By using gestures to reinforce the main points of your talk, you can make it more dynamic. Communications consultant Richard Southern advises that you "get your body involved in what you're saying." This will add power to your presentation and keep your audience involved from beginning to end.

*If your voice starts shaking, or if it begins
sounding like a whisper, speak louder."*

Dr. Morton Cooper,
—*Winning with Your Voice*

Be Prepared

In his book, *Inspire Any Audience*, Tony Jeary explains
that one way to overcome prespeech jitters is to
"know what you're talking about. Thorough preparation equals total confidence," he says. Some speakers
try "winging it" and hope for the best. But they often
fall flat on their faces and fail to impress the audience.
Preparation is the key to successful public speaking.

*It takes three weeks to prepare a good ad-lib
speech.*

—Mark Twain

PREPARATION

Melissa had to deliver a brief talk about her part-time
job at the print shop. She began by explaining how
she uses desktop publishing to design a brochure.
Then she described the process she followed to get
her job in the first place. Melissa spoke about her boss
and her co-workers. Next she discussed some of the

51

interesting projects she had completed for customers. Then she included something she forgot to say about desktop publishing. Finally, Melissa thanked her audience and sat down.

Melissa had spent very little time preparing her presentation. It had no central purpose. Consequently, it made little sense to her listeners. Unfortunately, many presentations sound the same way. "How many times have you sat through a presentation while all the time wondering to yourself, 'What is the speaker's main point?'" writes George Kops in *Great Speaches Aren't Born.*

In chapter 1, we talked about the *summary sentences* that define the purpose of your writing. The first step in preparing any good talk is to develop summary sentences that clearly define the purpose of your presentation.

FACTOID:

In the United States, an estimated 80,000 people stand up and speak before an audience every day.

Some speakers seem to confuse the *subject* and the *purpose* of their talk. The subject is usually quite broad. For instance, your boss might ask you to speak about the training course on computers that you just completed. With a subject that broad, you could say a great many things about it. A good talk, however, usually has a very sharply focused purpose. Listeners get overwhelmed if you try to tell them too much. The summary sentences define that purpose. They enable you to know and enable your listeners to know why you are speaking to them.

SAMPLE SUMMARY SENTENCES
Subject
The computer training course
Purpose
To *explain* how the course will help me on my job. My talk will give three examples of how I expect to use what I learned.
Subject
My volunteer work at the homeless shelter.
Purpose
To *persuade* other students to volunteer at the center. My talk will point out how this work benefits the homeless and how students can derive fulfillment from it.

Subject

My woodworking hobby

Purpose

To *describe* the process of making an item out of wood. My talk will discuss the important steps that I follow.

EXERCISE

For each of the following topics, develop a purpose for a talk. Write out the purpose in summary sentences.

1. A recent vacation

2. An especially difficult homework assignment

3. A part-time job after school

UNDERSTAND YOUR AUDIENCE

Crystal had been asked to speak to a group of customers who were taking a tour of her plant. She was supposed to talk about the area where she and the other members of her team worked.

"What will I say?" Crystal wondered. "I've never

given a talk like this before." Finally, she decided to discuss it with her supervisor.

"They're not technicians, like you are," Ms. Muniz, her supervisor, explained. "They don't need to know all the details of the manufacturing process."

"That's right, they're customers, aren't they?" Crystal said. "They want to be sure we're manufacturing quality products."

"Exactly," Ms. Muniz agreed. "So briefly describe how you carry out our quality process."

Remember what was said in chapter 1 about the importance of "writing for your reader?" The exact same principle applies to public speaking. The most important step in preparing any presentation is to understand your audience. "Before you start," advises Donald Walton in his book *Are You Communicating?* "it's wise to reflect on who your audience will be and what their primary interests are."

The most important step in preparing any presentation is to understand your audience.

LISTENER ANALYSIS

As you prepare a talk, conduct a *listener analysis*— analyze the people who are going to receive it. This is very similar to what you'd do before starting to write a memo or report. This information will help you determine what to say.

1. What do my listeners want to know about? If you don't give them information that interests them, you'll put them to sleep. Find out what they care about and cover this material in your talk.

2. How much do they already know? They may be experts or they may know almost nothing about your topic. You don't want to "talk down" to your listeners. But you also don't want to talk over their heads. Determine what your audience knows and pitch your talk to its level of understanding.

3. Where do they stand? Your listeners may be likely to agree with what you're saying or they may need a lot of convincing. Find out their attitudes, then determine what to say to persuade them of your point of view.

THE 3 Ts

One of the best ways of organizing any presentation is also the simplest. It's called the 3 Ts. You *tell* the audience what you're going to say to them *at the beginning* of your talk. Then you *tell* them *in the body.* Finally, you *tell* them what you told them in the conclusion. Let's explain this a little further.

Many speakers simply launch into a presentation

without ever explaining their purpose for speaking. They expect the audience to figure it out. Frequently, the audience doesn't or won't figure it out and they quickly lose interest.

FACTOID:

The attention span of most adults is about seven minutes.

At the beginning of your presentation, you should explain your purpose for speaking. This tells the audience why you are talking to them. You can almost literally present your summary sentences. "I want to explain how my computer training course will help me on the job. I'll give you three examples of how I expect to use what I learned." Now your listeners know what to expect. You won't lose their attention.

During the body of the talk, you tell them again. You discuss the three examples of how the course will help you. At the conclusion, you can repeat another version of the summary sentences. "As you can see, the course was extremely helpful. The three examples I've just discussed show you how I intend to use it." This leaves the purpose of your talk firmly fixed in the minds of your listeners.

At the beginning of your presentation, you should explain your purpose for speaking.

HOOK THE AUDIENCE

The 3 Ts provide a structure for your presentation. But by itself, a structure doesn't bring a presentation to life. Before a program begins, television producers like to present a *teaser*. This is something that hooks the viewers so they will keep watching. If it's a sit-com, the teaser may be a very funny scene from the story. If it's an adventure series, the teaser may be several action scenes from the show. Producers know that if viewers aren't hooked quickly, they may decide to channel surf.

Your audience is the same way. You have to hook their attention very quickly or they may tune out.

You can never be a great presenter without understanding and mastering strong openings.

—Frank Paolo,
How to Make a Great Presentation in 2 Hours

What types of openings work best? A story or anec-dote. A startling piece of information that no one has heard before. A newspaper headline. It should be something that will grab the interest of your listeners. It should also be something directly related to your purpose for speaking.

Gerald is the assistant manager of an electronics store in a shopping mall. He began a talk to his employees this way:

> Recently, I went to a store to buy some roller-blades. After looking at several different varieties, I had a few questions. I waited for a salesperson to come over and help me. There were very few people in the store, but I noticed that none of the three salespeople tried to help any of them. They stood in a corner drinking coffee together. Finally, I went over to see if I could get some help.
>
> "Excuse me," I said. "Could you answer some questions for me about your roller-blades?" One of the salespeople glared at me. "Look, you're interrupting an important discussion here," she said. "Don't be in such a hurry. We'll get to you in a few minutes."
>
> Well, I wasn't about to wait until she was ready. I turned around and walked out of the store.
>
> I'm telling you this story because it illustrates the purpose of my talk today: If we don't want to lose customers, we must learn how to satisfy them. And I want to explain how we do that.

Gerald began his talk with a personal anecdote that was closely tied to his purpose. The anecdote hooked his listeners. Then he could make an easy transition to his summary sentences. Gerald also might have started his presentation this way:

According to a recent survey, 53% of consumers said they would be shopping less this year, and 30% said they expect to spend less money shopping. What this means for us is that we have to do everything possible to hold on to our customers. To do that, we must always try to satisfy them. And in this talk I want to explain how we do that.

In this case, Gerald opened with a startling statistic that no one had probably heard before. Then he tied it directly to the purpose of his presentation.

SHOULD YOU OPEN WITH A JOKE?

Carol was giving a talk at parent's night in her school. She decided to begin with a joke, one that most of her friends found very funny. Unfortunately, she forgot that an audience of adults might be quite different from a group of her friends. As she completed the joke, Carol waited for everyone to laugh. Instead, there was stony silence. No one in the audience reacted. The joke had been a complete dud. What was worse, Carol had made a negative impression right from the beginning of her talk. As a result, no one in the audience was inclined to listen very closely to the rest of what she was saying.

"Humor is very high risk and I don't recommend it," explains communications consultant Granville Toogood." When an early joke goes flat, it tends to take all the bubbles out of whatever follows." For years, speakers opened their talks with a joke. But for many of them, it proved deadly. Sometimes the speaker wasn't a good story-teller. Or, as in Carol's case, her idea of what was funny wasn't the same as her audience's. Opening with an anecdote, an example, or an interesting fact is usually much more effective.

FACTOID:

Lincoln's Gettysburg Address is only 268 words long.

COMPLETING YOUR PRESENTATION

Talks don't have to be long to be effective. Lincoln's Gettysburg Address is a perfect example. It is perhaps the most memorable speech ever delivered by an American leader. The best talks should be concise as well as compelling. This means that the body, like the introduction, should contain interesting anecdotes

(Courtesy: U.S. Army Military History Institute)

In the Gettysburg Address—just 268 words in length—President Abraham Lincoln proved a speech can be both compelling and concise.

and examples. These things help bring your ideas to life and hold the attention of your audience. But always make sure that any information you present strengthens the purpose of your talk and supports your summary sentences.

Finally, repeat your purpose at the close of your talk. And if you can, illustrate it with an interesting story from your own experience or from something you've read. The more concrete and specific you can make a talk, the more likely your audience is to remember it.

PRACTICE MAKES (ALMOST) PERFECT

Creating a successful talk takes time. It involves developing a clear purpose, analyzing your audience, creating a structure for your talk and bringing it alive with interesting information. Once you have prepared the talk, put the key points on a few note cards. Then, rehearse it several times. This will enable you to become comfortable with the talk and improve your delivery. Preparation and practice will make you a better speaker.

THE 7+ SECRETS
OF SUCCESSFUL SPEAKING

1. Define the purpose of your presentation before doing anything else.

2. Spend plenty of time preparing your talk so it will be effective.

3. Hook the attention of your listeners early in a speech so they will listen to the rest of it.

4. Tell the audience why you're speaking to them at the beginning, the middle, and the end of your talk.

5. Overcome stage fright by making it work for you.

6. Use stories and anecdotes to bring your talk to life.

7. Evaluate each talk you give so you can constantly improve your skills.

7+. Never stop practicing.

EXERCISE

Complete one of the talks you were developing in the previous exercise. Make three main points in the body and support them with examples, interesting facts, or anecdotes. Create a conclusion that repeats the purpose of your presentation.

CHAPTER THREE
SPEAK WITH CONFIDENCE

3

"Good morning, Lisa," the interviewer said, extending his hand and smiling. Lisa rose as the short, round-faced man came toward her. She shook the interviewer's hand, but was afraid to look him directly in the eyes and turned her head away.

"Let's talk about your resume," the interviewer said. She followed him into his office and slumped into an upholstered chair in front of his desk. Lisa wondered what questions he might ask and whether she might be able to answer them.

"Well, what brings you to our company?" the interviewer began. "I mean, why do you want to work for us?"

"I saw your ad in the newspaper," Lisa said. "I've just graduated. And your job looked like it might be interesting."

"H'm," the interviewer replied. Lisa could tell her answer didn't really satisfy him. But what else did he expect her to say?

(Courtesy: Kelly Services)

Be friendly and speak with confidence when you interview for a job.

"Do you know what kind of work we do here?" the interviewer asked her.

"You're in the manufacturing business," Lisa said, proud of herself for having the answer.

"Well, it's a little more than that," the interviewer said sharply. "We're a leading toy maker. In fact, one of the biggest and best in the country."

He described some of the toys they manufactured and Lisa tried to appear interested. But she kept looking down at her hands and nervously twisting the ring on her little finger. As the interview continued, there were several other questions and Lisa tried hard to answer them. Unfortunately, she lacked confidence in herself and never seemed to find the right words. Finally, the interviewer said to her: "The job you're applying for is in marketing. What special skills would you bring to this position?"

Lisa knew this was important. The company wasn't going to hire just anybody. "Well, I took several business courses in school," she told him. "And I'm a hard worker. You can see by my resume, I've always had part-time jobs in school."

"Everyone who comes here works long hours," the interviewer told her. She could tell he wasn't very impressed with her answer. He glanced down at her resume again. "Do you have any other questions?"

"No, I don't think so," Lisa said. "When will I hear if I got the job?"

"We'll let you know," the interviewer told her. But as he rose and quickly escorted her to the door of his office, Lisa knew she didn't stand much of a chance of being hired.

JOB INTERVIEWS AND COMMUNICATION SKILLS

People fail to get hired because they lack effective communication skills.

In the work world, communication skills are critically important in many situations. These include job interviews, asking questions when you need help on an unfamiliar project, training other employees, and dealing with customers.

Job interviews like Lisa's occur every day. People fail to get hired because they lack effective communication skills. They simply don't know how to handle an interview. "It's 90% chemistry," explains executive recruiter Ron Pascel. "You need to get the interviewer to like you. Good interviewees will gauge the interviewers and figure out how to fit into their organization."

How do you accomplish these goals? Some tips from career counselors and human resource managers are:

▶ Do your homework.

▶ Know your purpose.

▶ Watch your body language.

▶ Be prepared.

Do Your Homework

Whenever you write, it's essential to know your reader. And if you stand up and give a talk, you should always know your listeners. This rule also applies in a job interview. Find out as much as you can about the organization where you're interviewing. An interviewer almost always will ask if you know something about his company. "Before you even shake an interviewer's hand, find out what the company does," advises Alicia Montecalvo in *Career World.* "Talk to friends or visit the library's reference section. Be sure the interviewer knows you've done your homework."

Know Your Purpose

Why do you go to a job interview? To persuade a company to hire you. But you can only accomplish this task by impressing interviewers with what you can do for their organizations. In short, take the *you* approach. What can I, as the interviewee, do for you, the employer. Your purpose is to sell the employer on you. And it's not enough to simply tell an employer you'll work hard, as Lisa did. Everyone is expected to do that. You have to do more.

"Know the job and the company," advises career counselor Rozanne Burt. "Then match what you found out to your skills."

If it's a marketing job for a toy company, explain how the courses you took in school taught you about selling to the consumer market. "You should also show your competencies in more than one sphere," Burt says. For example, your high grades in business courses may be one indication of your abilities. But you might also point out that you did volunteer work for a homeless shelter and helped them raise money. This also shows your marketing skills.

Watch Your Body Language

"Some interviewees look uninterested and don't pay attention when I talk," explains human resource director Debbie Berggren. "They look around my office. Consistent eye contact is important." Communication is not only verbal. It also involves body language. If you don't look at an interviewer when she shakes your hand, you make a very poor first

(Joe Duffy)

"I see you have experience in filing."

impression. Eye contact is also necessary during the interview. Looking at your hands, twisting your ring, or looking out the window communicates a lack of interest in the interviewer and the job.

Your body posture is important, too. If you recall, Lisa slouched in the chair. This suggested that she was not sharp and alert. Experts recommend that you sit up straight and lean slightly forward. This posture shows interviewers that you're listening closely to their questions and ready to answer them.

Be Prepared

"You can't over prepare for an interview," explains Pascel. His firm carefully goes over the questions job seekers are likely to be asked and helps prospective employees develop effective answers. "You want to be in control of the interview," he says. "You want to be in the driver's seat." It often helps to rehearse the interview, just as you'd rehearse a talk in front of an audience. Have a friend play the role of the interviewer and ask the types of questions posed to Lisa. For example, when the interviewer wants to know whether you have any questions about the job or the company, be prepared to say more than Lisa did. Ask about the types of projects you'll likely receive on the job, or the growth potential and the opportunity to assume greater responsibilities. This shows that you've thought about the position and your own career goals.

By following these four tips, you usually can improve your interviewing skills. You'll go into an interview feeling more confident and you'll communicate this confidence to the interviewer. This will make it more likely that you will be offered a job.

DOS AND DON'TS
OF JOB INTERVIEWS

► Do bring your resume because the interviewer will want to see it.

► Don't bring any of your friends for moral support because the interviewer doesn't want to talk to them.

► Do speak clearly because the interviewer will not be impressed if you mumble your words.

► Don't give the interviewer a limp-wristed handshake because it may indicate that you are an ineffective employee.

► Do show enthusiasm for the job or the interviewer will think you don't want it.

► Don't respond to the interviewer's questions with a blank stare; be prepared with good answers.

► Don't slouch or drape yourself over the chair—poor posture suggests to an interviewer that you are not sharp and alert.

► Do look the interviewer in the eye when you speak, otherwise he may think you have something to hide.

EXERCISE

The best way to learn more about job interviewing is to talk to people who know about it.

► Ask friends who are currently working about the types of questions they were asked in their interviews and how they answered them.

► Talk to local employers and find out what questions they ask in job interviews and the answers they expect to receive from potential employees.

QUESTIONS CAN MAKE THE DIFFERENCE

David was hired by a health care company to work in their customer service department. He enjoyed talking to people, giving them information and even handling their complaints. As part of his job, David also was expected to publish a quarterly customer newsletter. This meant that he had to understand desktop publishing. While he had seen some materials produced with desktop publishing in school, David hadn't actually produced any himself. But he thought when the time came, he'd figure it out. As employees submitted their articles for the newsletter,

David let them sit in a pile on his desk. The deadline for the first newsletter came and went, and David's manager kept asking him when it was going to be published.

"I'll have it for you soon," David promised. But when he tried using the desktop publishing system, he couldn't figure it out. He even bought a book that explained desktop publishing in simple language. It was no use, he simply did not understand the instructions.

David was in a panic. If he asked someone for help, his boss might find out. But if he didn't produce the newsletter, his boss might get very angry. Perhaps even fire him. What should he do?

For a new employee, the ability to ask the right questions may be the most important communication skill you can possess. "Don't be afraid or too proud to ask for help," explains Bradley Richardson, author of *Job Smarts for Twentysomethings.*

Don't be afraid or too proud to ask for help.

"How dumb will you look when you had the resources all around you, but dropped the ball because you were too afraid of looking stupid?" Richardson adds.

When you just start a job, or are asked to take on an unfamiliar assignment, no one expects you to know everything. And yet many employees are timid about asking questions. Others, who might have performed very well at school, may feel that they know everything. They don't think they need to ask for help.

Ask the Three Key Questions

1. How do I do it?

2. When does it have to be done?

3. Why does it have to be done?

How Do I Do It? This is the most important question to ask. But it's often far less simple than it sounds.

Suppose you're trying to put out a newsletter using desktop publishing, as David was assigned to do. Don't panic. Instead, you might start by doing some background reading to determine what you understand about the process and what you don't. Perhaps there are some new terms that seem unclear to you. The steps you need to follow in developing graphics and laying out pages also may seem mystifying. Figuring out what you don't know and making a list of questions for yourself is the best way to start coming up with the information you need. Then find someone to provide you with answers. It may be a

(Courtesy: Michael Conroy, MacNeil/Lehrer Productions)

Jim Lehrer of the Newshour *on PBS, is a successful interviewer because he isn't afraid to ask guests to rephrase their answers in plain English so that his viewers can understand them.*

coworker in your own department. If not, perhaps one of your coworkers can suggest someone else in another part of the organization. Make an appointment to talk to that individual, then show up with all your questions.

If, at first, the answer to one of your questions doesn't seem clear, ask for further explanation. One of the best approaches for finding out information is demonstrated nightly by Jim Lehrer on the *Newshour,* which is aired by most PBS stations. Lehrer insists that every guest he interviews put their answers in plain language that any viewer can understand. He also is not afraid to appear uninformed if he doesn't quite understand what the guest means. Lehrer simply asks him to state it again more simply. This is the same approach you should use when asking for information.

When Does It Have to be Done? You should always ask your supervisor about the deadline for completing the project. But there are other questions you might ask, as well. Is the final deadline flexible? Some projects have a fixed deadline. For example, a presentation for the national sales meeting has to be ready by the day of the meeting. For other projects, however, your supervisor might be willing to extend the deadline if necessary. You might also ask if there are "milestones" in the completion of the project. Does your supervisor expect to see a rough draft of the newsletter by a specific date so he can give you his comments? These milestones will help you plan a project more carefully so it will always be done by the deadline.

Why Does It Have to be Done? "Don't just learn how to do something," advises author Bradley Richardson, "learn why you do something!" Why is a newsletter important to the customers? How does your newsletter help other parts of the organization, like the sales department? Learning the "whys" enables you to understand the importance of a project and strengthens your commitment to it.

ASKING GOOD QUESTIONS: STEP BY STEP

1. Figure out in advance what you don't know and what you need to know.

2. Find out from a friend or coworker who is most likely to have the answers you need.

3. Make an appointment to see that person, especially if she is a busy supervisor.

4. State each question as clearly and simply as possible.

5. Don't become flustered if the individual asks for clarification—put your question in different words and ask it again.

6. If at first you don't understand the answer, don't be afraid to ask for more information.

7. Thank the individual for taking time to answer your questions.

ONE-TO-ONE: HELPING OTHER EMPLOYEES

After you've gained some experience on a job, you may be the one assigned to train new employees. Charlene Richards works after school as an aide at a nature center. "Whenever I'm training new employees," she says, "I don't assume anything. Maybe they know a great deal; maybe they know nothing. First, I find out if they've ever had any experience doing this kind of work. If they have, then I figure they already understand something about how to care for animals. If they haven't, then I show them everything, every little detail."

Charlene tries to understand her listeners. She puts herself in their place and asks, "What would they want to know?" She can also remember her first days on the job, how nervous she was at learning everything, and how important it was to have someone explain it to her carefully.

"I know I asked a lot of dumb questions," she recalls. Fortunately, her supervisor was very patient and answered each one of them.

Charlene has prepared her training program thoroughly. There are a few key points that she repeats again and again throughout the presentation. One of these is to always follow the feeding directions on each animal's cage. She begins with an example to make her point. Charlene shows the trainees the two ferrets that currently live in the nature center and explains why they need different types of food. Cleaning the cages regularly is also important. Finally, volunteers should be alert to any signs of unusual behavior by the animals.

During the program Charlene communicates an attitude of openness through her body language. She smiles frequently and maintains eye contact. After the program is over, Charlene regards herself as a resource for the volunteers. She wants to be someone they can turn to for advice while they're doing their jobs.

"It's only common sense," she says. "If you want people to do a good job, you have to give them as much support as possible. And that takes good communication." Careful preparation, a clear purpose, an understanding of your listeners, and effective use of body language—these are key elements of successful communication.

THE KEYS TO HELPING OTHERS ON THE JOB

▶ Practice empathy—putting yourself in another person's shoes and understanding how he feels.

▶ Communicate your ideas clearly.

▶ Listen carefully to what other people want.

▶ Don't call any question a "dumb" question; answer it.

▶ Let people know that you like them.

▶ Tell people that you're there if they need you.

▶ Don't say you know an answer if you don't—find out the information and get back to people with it later.

EXERCISE

Select a part-time job or after-school activity. Outline your explanation of how to do the job or activity to someone who knows nothing about it. Emphasize the main points necessary to do it successfully. Deliver an oral presentation based on the outline. Ask your parents or a close friend to listen and give you feedback on it.

COMMUNICATING WITH CUSTOMERS

Effective communication is important not only with other people inside your organization but also with people from the outside as well. No matter what job you hold—manufacturing or marketing, finance or public relations—you may come in contact with customers. And the impression you make tells them a great deal about your organization.

Effective communication is important not only with other people inside your organization but also with people from the outside as well.

"My first impression of a company is the receptionist," says career counselor John Jarvis. He explains that he often calls a company to obtain information on its products and services to help his students who might want to apply for positions there. "If the receptionist can't explain what the company does, she will always remain a receptionist. But, someone who puts the company in a good light will go on and get promotions to more responsible positions."

This is exactly what happened to Barbara. She started as a receptionist, answering the phone at a small insurance company.

"Customers would call with a problem," she said. "I'd try to put myself in their place and be as pleasant as possible, even though some of them were not always very nice. But I knew they needed to talk with one of our insurance representatives, so I'd route them to the right person as quickly as I could."

Eventually Barbara completed college and took on more responsibilities. She administered the company's benefits program and wrote its annual report. She was promoted to human resources manager. Today she interviews people seeking employment and conducts orientation programs for new employees. The orientation program enables new hires to learn about the company's benefits and other policies. Barbara also supervises a staff of three people.

"Communications," she says, "has always been a major part of my job."

Barbara started working her way up the organization because she knew how to deal with customers in her first position as a receptionist. Sometimes it's easy to forget that no company can stay in business for very long, unless it knows how to satisfy its customers and treat them properly.

The general manager of a hotel once explained that customers get their first impression of his organization when they telephone for reservations. "If the person on the other end of the telephone isn't courteous," he said, "the customer immediately thinks badly of our entire hotel."

The same thing might be said for many types of service jobs. The teller at a bank, the person standing behind the counter in a fast food restaurant, the cashier at a supermarket—all of them leave a lasting impression on customers. Indeed, they are often the only people who directly communicate with customers.

So, if you hold one of these positions, you're responsible for what the customer thinks of the company where you work. You also have an impact on whether they will return to your company to do business again. Remember, you not only make an impres-

---

WHEN YOU WORK, REMEMBER THE CUSTOMER

1. The customers pay your salary, they have a right to your courtesy.

2. The customers should always receive the highest quality you can give them.

3. The customer's first impression is usually a lasting one.

4. Customer service should always be your top priority.

5. Customers deserve a smile as well as a kind word.

6. Customers are the most valuable asset a business possesses.

---

sion on customers with your words. Body language is also important. A ready smile, direct eye contact, and a firm handshake are communication skills that will win you high marks whenever you deal with customers.

A ready smile, direct eye contact, and a firm handshake are communication skills that will win you high marks whenever you deal with customers.

COMMUNICATIONS—A CRITICAL SKILL

Whether you're interviewing for a job, learning the ropes on a new position, training other employees or talking with customers, you need to be a good communicator. Developing confidence in your abilities as an oral communicator takes practice. If you don't prepare for a job interview, for example, you probably won't get hired. Asking the right questions is another essential skill, even if it means exposing your ignorance. It isn't easy, but it's often what you must do to be successful on a job.

Communication not only involves your verbal skills, but your body language as well. Your posture, your eye contact, and your facial expressions leave an impression on your listeners—one that is just as significant as what you say to them. Remember, always keep your listeners in mind when you communicate. They're the ones you need to impress.

CHAPTER FOUR
IS ANYBODY LISTENING?

4

Jeff was a brilliant student. He graduated from college with a 3.8 GPA and a degree in engineering. After graduation, he received job offers from a variety of prestigious companies. Finally, he decided to go to work for a well-known manufacturing firm in the Midwest.

Jeff was immediately assigned to one of the teams that developed new products. The team was made up of engineers and designers as well as people from manufacturing, sales, and marketing. Jeff would have a unique opportunity to work in one of the most exciting areas of the company. And he would learn product development from the firm's most experienced team.

Unfortunately, Jeff was not much of a team player. In college, he liked working on his own and taking all the credit for whatever he accomplished. On a team, it was different. At team meetings, he was expected to cooperate with his coworkers and listen to what they had to say. Jeff found these situations very difficult.

"I think we may need to consider some changes in the design of this product," said one of the manufacturing supervisors at a recent team meeting. "I'm not sure..."

But Jeff cut him off before he could finish. "What do you mean?" he said. "I think this design will work just fine." The other members of the team were stunned. How could a young engineer with almost no experience be so arrogant?

"There he goes again," one of the salespeople whispered. "He's never going to last at this company. He just won't listen to anyone."

THE ROLE OF TEAMWORK

Today teams do much of the work inside organizations. Teams may operate inside a single area of a company, like sales or finance. They may also involve several different areas, or functions, like Jeff's team.

The people who run organizations realize that to create and sell a new product, they need input from employees with many types of expertise. In the past, these individuals might have worked on their own in different parts of the company. Today they are all brought together on teams. These cross-functional teams, as they are called, may not only conceptualize a new product, they also may figure out how to manufacture it, and finally how to market it to customers. This frequently means a product can be developed quicker and cheaper than in the past.

For a team to work smoothly, its members must be able to communicate effectively. They must speak clearly and concisely so everyone understands what they are saying. They must also be willing to listen and learn from each other. Otherwise nothing can be accomplished.

FIVE RULES FOR EFFECTIVE LISTENING

1. Don't interrupt.

2. Don't jump to conclusions.

3. Don't judge the messenger, evaluate the message.

4. Put yourself in the speaker's place.

5. Don't tune out, find something of interest.

Don't Interrupt

How many times has someone interrupted what you're trying to say? Perhaps it was one of your parents, or a friend, or even a coworker. Chances are you felt pretty irritated. You may also have wondered why that person was acting so rudely. Some people don't mean to be rude. They just can't seem to control themselves. They are so eager to say something, to express their opinion, that they simply can't wait for the speaker to finish.

"People fail to understand about half of what they hear. And they quickly forget half of that."
Donald Walton, *Are You Communicating?*

Teams can't function efficiently if resentment has built up between different members.

Unfortunately, teams don't operate very well in this kind of environment. Everyone deserves an equal chance to be heard. If an employee is cut off in mid-sentence, interrupted while she is presenting an important idea, she is likely to feel unappreciated. She may even begin to resent the coworker who interrupts her. Teams can't function efficiently if resentment has built up between different members. Imagine trying to run a basketball team where the players didn't get along with each other. The spirit of teamwork would disappear and the team might stop trying to win.

Interrupting, as Jeff did, might also prevent an employee from saying something vital to the future of the team and the success of its project. Teams that operate best give everyone a chance to make a contribution.

FACTOID:

According to one study, we listen with only 25% efficiency. This accounts for many of the misunderstandings that occur on the job.

Don't Jump to Conclusions

Allison worked at Fairway Cleaners for a few hours each week after school and on Saturdays. When customers came in, she took their cleaning and wrote up a ticket for it. The ticket had to include every item that belonged to the customer and indicate the exact day when they wanted to have their cleaning ready to pick up. Accuracy was important.

"Good morning, Mrs. Carlson," Allison said with a smile. "That's a big load of cleaning this week." Mrs. Carlson was an old customer who had been coming in for as long as Allison had worked at Fairway. She usually left her cleaning on Saturday and wanted it a week later.

"Summer vacation," Mrs. Carlson said. "Our family goes through a lot of clothing, and my husband has a business trip next Thursday." She put the pants in one pile, shirts in another and sweaters in a third. "I think there are five pairs of pants," Mrs. Carlson began.

But Allison was already moving ahead of her. She was counting the pants herself and putting this information on the ticket, then the shirts and finally the sweaters. On the ticket, she also indicated that the cleaning would be ready in a week, the way Mrs. Carlson always wanted it.

Then Allison handed her the ticket. "Have a nice weekend."

"Thanks, Allison," Mrs. Carlson said. "I'll see you in a few days."

"That's funny," Allison thought. "It'll be a whole week before I see her again. Maybe she just got confused."

Late Wednesday afternoon, Allison came into the cleaners after her last class. There was Mrs. Carlson, and she was talking to Allison's boss. "There's been a terrible mistake," he said angrily. "Mrs. Carlson specifically told you that this cleaning was supposed to be ready on Wednesday. Now, she's stopped in on her way home from work and it isn't here. Her husband's leaving on a business trip tomorrow and he needs these clothes."

(V. Harlow/Higganum Drug Center)

It's important for a store clerk to listen carefully and concentrate when customers make comments.

Allison didn't know what to say. "I...I just assumed, Mrs. Carlson. I mean you always want your cleaning on Saturday." Her boss was very upset. "You've got to pay attention, Allison! That's if you want to keep working here."

FACTOID:

The average speaker talks at about 160 words per minute, but we can absorb information at three times that rate.

Since we can process information much faster than someone speaks it's easy to stop paying attention to the speaker and begin thinking about something else. That's exactly what happened to Allison. Her mind leapt ahead and she didn't listen to Mrs. Carlson. Allison assumed she knew what Mrs. Carlson was going to say, and she jumped to the wrong conclusion.

Whenever you receive instructions on a job, it's important to listen carefully. Don't assume you know what the speaker is going to say, and stop paying attention. If a customer is asking you to do something, listen to everything he has to say. If your boss is speaking, listen until she finishes and don't jump to the wrong conclusion. Good listening skills will enable you to be a better employee.

EXERCISE

Are you a good listener? If you can answer "yes" to these questions, then you have effective listening skills. If not, you probably need to work harder.

1. I usually allow a speaker to finish talking without interrupting.

2. I don't jump to conclusions when someone is talking, but listen carefully.

(Continued on next page)

(Excercise continued)

3. I don't evaluate a speaker by the way she looks or sounds, I listen to the message.

4. I try to put myself in the speaker's shoes and treat her the way I would want to be treated.

5. I concentrate on the speaker and don't let distractions get in the way.

6. If I disagree with someone, I hold my comments until she stops talking.

7. When I'm listening, I listen to the speaker's tone of voice and look at her body language.

8. When somone speaks, I usually try to look for something valuable in what she's saying.

DON'T JUDGE THE MESSENGER, EVALUATE THE MESSAGE

Sometimes we let our attitudes about the speaker prevent us from listening carefully to what is being said. One manager from the Northeast explained that she was used to dealing with people who speak quickly and that she likes to talk pretty fast herself. She admitted that whenever she has to listen to someone who talks slowly, she begins to get impatient and even stops listening. "Why can't they just get to the point?" she says.

Whether we like to admit it or not, each of us has certain biases. And these may get in the way of effective listening. Some common biases are:

► How does the speaker sound?

► How does the speaker look?

► How old is the speaker?

How Does the Speaker Sound? If the person has an unfamiliar accent, we may find ourselves prejudging what she is going to say without really listening to her. Perhaps she comes from a different region of the country or a different part of the world. Perhaps she speaks more slowly than we do, or more quickly. None of these is a valid reason to jump to conclusions and dismiss what the speaker may say before we give her a fair chance.

How Does the Speaker Look? The first thing you notice about people is their appearance. What kind of clothes do they have? How much jewelry do they wear? It's easy to let someone's appearance—especially someone who looks different from you—stand in the way of effective communication. In his book, *Are You Communicating?* Donald Walton points out that this is one of the emotional obstacles that can

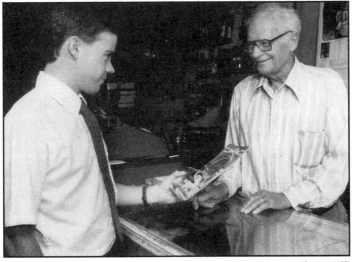

(Courtesy: AARP)

Even though there may be a big age difference between you and a customer, always focus on what is being said, not how old the person is.

prevent you from giving rational consideration to what someone is saying.

Suppose the supermarket where you work hires a new cashier who is assigned the checkout counter next to yours. He's done this kind of work before and offers you some suggestions that might make your job easier. But you think he looks weird, so you don't listen. Walton urges that you concentrate instead on what the speaker is saying rather than who is saying it. "Is it true? Does it sound right to me? Is it contrary

99

to or in line with the facts that I've previously heard?" Walton says that these are the issues you should be thinking about. Don't get hung up on appearances.

How Old Is the Speaker? Age is sometimes an enormous barrier to effective communication. If a person has gray hair, it's easy to assume that he can't relate to you. And some adults feel that a teenager is too young, and too inexperienced to teach them anything. This is another example of an emotional generalization that can prevent effective listening. Instead, each messenger and each message must be evaluated on their own merits.

Age is sometimes an enormous barrier to effective communication.

EXERCISE

Can you think of a situation when you unfairly evaluated what a speaker was saying because of his age, or accent, or the way he looked? Write several paragraphs describing what happened. How could you avoid this problem in the future?

PUT YOURSELF IN THE SPEAKER'S PLACE

Corey works as an assistant at a large veterinary hospital. Clients bring in their pets not only for routine visits, but also for serious illnesses and major operations. Corey assists the veterinarian with many kinds of services to the animals.

"It's important to understand why the animal is there and what the owner is feeling," Corey explains. "If the client is worried, I pick up on that. I listen to what they say and watch their body language. Then I try to make small talk to help them feel better."

Sometimes a client will call the hospital after a pet has undergone surgery to find out how the animal is doing. "If the doctor is busy," Corey explains, " I may take the call and talk to the customer. I know they're worried and I try to understand that. I give them all the information I can. I tell them how the animal is feeling, whether the anesthesia has worn off—anything that will reassure the owner that their pet is all right."

Good listeners have the ability to empathize with a speaker. They try to read the speaker's body language, just as Corey did. Perhaps the speaker has a pained expression on his face, holds himself tensely or rubs his hands continuously. Any of these clues may indicate that he is very nervous. His halting style of speech or emotional tone of voice may also indicate that he is upset.

Listeners can then use what management consultant Ron Meis calls "openers" and "encouragers" to enable the speaker to communicate more easily. The listener might say, "It looks to me that there's something you'd like to talk about," or "Is there something bothering you?" Openers, like these, may get the speaker started. Listeners can also communicate their interest in what the speaker is saying by nodding their heads, making eye contact with the speaker or using phrases such as "that's interesting." These skills encourage the speaker to keep talking.

FACTOID:

How do we communicate a message? Only 7% of our message comes through the words we use; 38% comes through our tone of voice; and 55% comes through our body language.

DON'T TUNE OUT,
FIND SOMETHING OF INTEREST

In school, we are required to sit through many hours of classes. On the job, we will be required to sit through many meetings and training sessions. If we allow ourselves to get bored and start daydreaming, chances are we won't listen very carefully to what's being said. How do you beat boredom?

One way to is to look for something of value in

what the speaker is saying—something that can benefit you. Suppose you've just gone to work at a new company, and you're sitting through a two-day orientation program. Speakers from various departments talk about their operations and how they contribute to the company's success. These programs can be long and tedious, if you approach them that way. Or they can give you a chance to find out where you might eventually like to work in the organization. Perhaps one department sounds particularly interesting with plenty of opportunity for growth. This might be the place for you to set your sights.

"We have two ears and one mouth, that we might listen twice as much as we speak."
Epictetus, Greek writer

To stay focused during a long presentation, it also helps to take notes. You don't have to worry about all the details. It's enough to listen for the main ideas and write them down. This will help you to concentrate and enable you to avoid distractions. Some presentations are followed by question-and-answer sessions. It's often a good idea to formulate questions

To stay focused during a long presentation, it also helps to take notes.

while you are listening to the speaker. This is another way to concentrate on what he is saying, avoid boredom and focus your attention on the main ideas. Good questions will provide you with additional information. They'll also give you a way to stand out from most of your peers and show your superiors that you are listening carefully to what they're saying.

LISTENING IS ACTIVE, NOT PASSIVE

Some people think that listening is a passive activity, much like watching television. But it's not. Good listening means an active involvement in the communication process. It involves an ability to empathize with the speaker, listen to the speaker's words and read his body language. It requires a willingness to look past appearances, overcome our biases and evaluate the speaker's message. It demands that we let the speaker speak without interrupting or jumping to conclusions. Finally, good listening means that we must concentrate on what the speaker is saying, looking for value in it and avoiding distractions.

EXERCISE

The next time you listen to someone speak in school or at work, practice the skills of active listening. Grade yourself from 1 to 5, poor to excellent, on how well you practice each skill.

▶ Letting the speaker talk, without interrupting or jumping to conclusions

▶ Empathizing with the speaker

▶ Evaluating the message, not the messenger

▶ Finding value in what is being said

▶ Concentrating on the speaker and avoiding distractions

▶ Asking meaningful questions

CHAPTER FIVE
MAKING MEETINGS WORK

Harold leaned back in his seat and sighed wearily. The assistant sales manager had been talking steadily for almost 25 minutes and showed no signs of slowing down. "Why does he always go on so long?" Harold wondered. "He just puts all of us to sleep."

Slowly, Harold began tuning out his boss's presentation as his mind wandered to more pleasant topics. He thought about the vacation that was coming up soon. Harold had reservations at a beautiful hotel on the beach. And he was planning to spend the entire week without his beeper or cellular phone.

"I won't have to hear the boss's voice for seven days," Harold thought. "What could be more wonderful?"

His mind then drifted on to the big sale he'd just completed yesterday. The customer had more than doubled her usual order. A smile crossed Harold's lips. "Yes," he nodded to himself, "that was a job well done."

(Joe Duffy)

"Nobody gives a better report than Collins."

Suddenly, Harold's daydreaming was interrupted. "Harold," his boss said with a hearty laugh, "I want to thank you for nodding your head and volunteering to take on this important project."

Harold was stunned. He turned to one of his co-workers at the meeting. "What project?" he whispered.

"Writing the big report that's due in two weeks," she said. "But, I can't," Harold told him. "I'm going on vacation."

108

"No, you're not," he smiled. "It just got canceled."

MEETINGS...MEETINGS...MEETINGS

In business, meetings are a fact of life. Project teams get together for meetings. Salespeople meet with customers. New employees meet for training sessions. According to consultants Roger Mosvick and Robert Nelson, the number of business meetings is growing. But that doesn't mean they're getting more done. Indeed, Mosvick and Nelson report that "over 50 % of the productivity of billions of meeting hours is wasted." Why? Poor meeting preparation, they explain, and lack of training on how to conduct meetings effectively. As a result, employees like Harold tend to tune out and fail to participate.

FACTOID:

Managers and professionals in organizations spend ¼ of their week in meetings.

A well-run meeting combines the writing, speaking, and listening skills that we've been discussing in this book. Whether you're leading a meeting, or just a participant, you need to communicate clearly.

Whether you're leading a meeting, or just a participant, you need to communicate clearly.

EXERCISE

Think about the last meeting you attended.
What was the purpose of the meeting? Did all
the people who attended need to be there? Did
the meeting last longer than necessary? What
did you get out of the meeting?

WHAT'S ON THE AGENDA?

*A group of seniors was meeting to talk about the class
prom. It was the third time that all of them had come
together. The discussion went on for two hours. It was
a free-for-all, with everybody expressing their opinions.
But by the end of the meeting, there was still no
agreement on what they should do for the prom.*

*In a large office building, a group of managers sat
around discussing the annual company outing. They
talked and talked. They traded stories about past
company outings. Then they complained to each other
about problems in their departments. Finally, they
started to wonder whether there should be an outing
at all this year. After three hours, nothing had been
accomplished. And all the arrangements for having*

the outing were supposed to be finalized by the end of the week.

Meetings can often become long-winded talk fests where nothing is ever accomplished. One way to avoid this problem is to carefully structure the meeting. That structure is called an "agenda." As authors Richard Chang and Kevin Kehoe explain, "Just as the developer works from a blueprint and shares it with other people working on the building, a meeting should have a 'blueprint'....The blueprint for any meeting is its agenda, which provides everyone with a picture of what the meeting will look like."

Perhaps the most critical element of any agenda is the meeting objective. If you're leading a meeting, one of your responsibilities is to set the objectives. These comprise the purpose of the meeting. Just as when you're writing a memo or report, your first job is to determine its purpose, and you express the purpose in your summary sentences.

Agenda for a Meeting

1. Objectives

2. Logistics—date, time, place, participants

3. Preparation

4. Activities

When developing an agenda, write a sentence for each objective. These short sentences tell the participants what you want to cover in the meeting and what you hope to accomplish. In this way, you can avoid a rambling meeting that goes off in the wrong direction. Those are meetings that usually accomplish nothing.

Suppose you're in charge of planning the class prom. Your meeting's objective might be: *To generate a list of four possible places to hold the prom.*

Your next step would be to set a date, time, and place for the meeting. Punctuality is important. If people are wandering in late, it only disrupts and drags out the meeting. Sometimes you even find yourself having to explain important points all over again for their benefit, wasting precious time. In business meetings, your boss may be a stickler for punctuality. As one manager put it: "If they show up five minutes late, I usually tell them to forget it."

PEOPLE AND PREPARATION

In a study of executives conducted by the Wharton Center for Applied Research at the University of Pennsylvania, a majority reported that there were too many people at meetings. And a large number of them did not need to be there, nor did they make any meaningful contribution. When a meeting becomes unwieldy, far less is accomplished. Only invite those people who absolutely have to attend. Give them the agenda in advance if you want them to do any preparation for the meeting. Suppose you want someone to report on the place where the prom was held by last year's senior class. This information might be important in enabling your group to make a selection for this year's prom. Or perhaps you want participants to read an article that appeared in a magazine in the school library which lists the elements of successful school proms. If participants receive the agenda in advance, they can do all the necessary preparation. This will enable the meeting to be far more productive.

A report from the Annenberg School of Communications at the University of Southern California explains that most meetings occur "with only two hours' notice and ...no written agenda, or, if it has an agenda, the meeting often fails to cover it...." As a result, the meetings often seem ineffective. You can avoid this problem by carefully developing a set of objectives, defining the logistics of the meeting, limiting participants and insisting that they do their preparation.

Finally, your agenda should list the meeting's activities. These are designed to carry out the objectives of the meeting. As the leader, you may want to make a brief presentation at the beginning. This might be followed by the report on last year's prom. There might also be a discussion of the article that you asked everybody to read. Then everyone might discuss possible locations for this year's event. Finally, a small committee might be appointed to investigate these locations and make a report at the next meeting.

EXERCISE

1. **What meetings have you attended lately? How would you rate them in terms of accomplishing their objectives? How could these meetings have been improved?**

2. **Think about a meeting that you're planning to lead in the near future. Copy the meeting agenda form and fill in the information described in this section of the chapter: objectives; date, time, location; participants; preparation; activities.**

FILL IN THE BLANKS.
Meeting Agenda

Objectives: _____

_____

_____

Date: _____ Time: _____

Location: _____

Participants: _____

_____

Preparation: _____

_____

_____

Activities: _____

   1. _____

   2. _____

   3. _____

   4. _____

YOU'RE THE SPEAKER

Suppose you have to lead a meeting of your work team. First, you'll probably need to make a short presentation at the beginning of the meeting, welcoming participants and explaining the agenda. This requires effective speaking skills. As you begin the talk, explain your objectives clearly. And be sure you add energy to your delivery.

The best way to develop interest and enthusiasm in your listeners is by using energy.
— **George Kops**

Energy can keep people involved and prevent them from daydreaming or even falling asleep.

If you've ever heard speakers who talk in a dull monotone, you know how boring it can be. Energy can keep people involved and prevent them from daydreaming or even falling asleep. You can add energy with your voice by emphasizing certain words or ideas as you speak to indicate they are very important. By changing volume—making your voice louder or softer—you add variety to your presentation.

Gestures are another way of adding energy. As you talk, use your hands to reinforce what you're saying. If you're listing three objectives, use your fingers to indicate the first, second, and the third points. If you're making a key point, try jabbing the air with your forefinger. Or if you're asking support from participants at the meeting, stretch out your hands to them. Gestures automatically raise the vocal energy

(Courtesy: Kelly Services)

To be an effective speaker, making gestures with your hands is an energetic approach to hold the interest of an audience. By using your hands, you emphasize key words and phrases, keeping the listeners focused on what you have to say.

of your talk. In fact if you use gestures, it's almost impossible to speak in a monotone.

As we've mentioned earlier, making eye contact with your listeners is another way to keep them involved. As you begin a thought, look at one listener. Continue looking at that listener, until you complete the thought. Then, select another listener and repeat the process. This enables you to establish a dialogue

117

with every participant. And that's an effective way to keep them focused on what you're saying.

Nothing builds rapport faster than eye contact. Building rapport is critical for achieving audience buy-in—and without 100% buy-in, it's terribly difficult to inspire an audience to act.
        —**Tony Jeary,** *Inspire Any Audience*

EXERCISE

The next time you stand up and speak at a meeting, grade yourself on your use of energy. Rate yourself from 1 to 5, poor to excellent.

1. Did you speak with enthusiasm?

2. Did you raise your voice level to emphasize certain words?

3. Did you use gestures to reinforce your ideas?

4. Did you make eye contact with each of your listeners?

5. Did you keep your listeners involved in the meeting?

REMEMBERING YOUR LISTENING SKILLS

Whether you're a meeting leader or a participant, listening is just as important as speaking. Mosvick and Nelson emphasize that leaders should not try to dominate a meeting, but should involve the other participants. This means that every leader must be able to listen. Participants should also give each other the courtesy of listening without interrupting.

Listening is just as important as speaking.

As this book explained earlier, you can listen at a much faster rate than you speak. If you're not careful, this can create problems. Suppose you work in your company's customer service department. You're sitting at a meeting where one of your colleagues is presenting her plan to serve customers more rapidly. Part way through her presentation, you decide that her plan won't work. But instead of listening to the rest of it, you immediately begin to write out a rebuttal. By not listening to the rest of her plan, you may miss some key points. These may persuade you that her plan actually will work. At the very least, listening may help you shape a better rebuttal. By listening to each of her main points, you can rebut all, instead of some, of them.

Every rebuttal should be presented as respectfully as possible. That is, you must know how to disagree with others politely. If you think someone's idea won't work, it does no good to say "that's stupid!" This type of comment simply insults your colleague. The goal of a meeting is not to demonstrate your own intelligence by "one-upping" someone else. This just engenders hard feelings. The goal of each meeting is to create a synergy among the participants. This means that by working together you should be able to increase each other's effectiveness.

It's almost impossible to work together, however, if a meeting is being torn apart by serious disagreements. These must be handled very carefully.

Find something positive to say about another employee's proposal, even if you disagree with it.

First, find something positive to say about another employee's proposal, even if you disagree with it. By starting on a positive note, you can demonstrate at least some support for your coworker. You can also show your appreciation for the hard work they have put into their proposal.

Second, don't come on too strong. Present your disagreement gently. Use phrases such as "I think" or "Maybe, we should consider," or "Perhaps there's another way to look at this." Don't sound like a know-it-all.

Third, enlist support from other people at the meeting. After you've presented your ideas, ask them what they think. Often the leader will step in at this point and ask other people at the meeting to express their views. This may enable everyone to reach some general agreement.

CONCLUDING THE MEETING

As Richard Chang and Kevin Kehoe point out, the leader's role is to make sure the meeting follows the agenda. A meeting that stays on track is less likely to consume needless time. A leader is also responsible for reviewing any decisions and actions that are taken at a meeting. A review makes certain that everyone fully understands the decisions and actions.

Many meetings conclude with one or more action steps. This often ensures that a meeting accomplishes a meaningful goal. Suppose you and your colleagues at the customer service meeting decide on these two action steps to improve service. First, you will answer customer calls after only a single ring of the telephone. Second, if you don't know the answer to a customer's question, you will find out by the next business day. All of you agree to carry out these steps and report the results at the next meeting.

Generally, participants try to reach a consensus on their decisions and actions. This process is easier in a meeting where the spirit of cooperation prevails. If everyone feels they have been heard and their opinions respected, they are far more likely to reach agreement.

WHAT MAKES A MEETING SUCCESSFUL?

1. A clear agenda which is available to participants in advance.

2. A list of attendees which includes only those people essential to the meeting.

3. A date, time and place for the meeting.

4. A leader who uses effective speaking skills in running the meeting.

5. A willingness among everyone to listen attentively while others are speaking.

6. The ability to handle disagreements successfully.

7. A set of clear action steps to follow up the meeting.

Everyone has a right to, and an obligation for, simplicity and clarity in communication. We owe each other truth and courtesy, though truth is sometimes a real constraint, and courtesy inconvenient. But make no mistake—these are the qualities that allow communication to educate and liberate us.

—**Max DePrese**, *Leadership is an Art*

MEETINGS REQUIRE ALL YOUR SKILLS

Successful meetings don't just happen. They require all the skills we've been discussing in this book. Clear, concise writing is a key element of a focused agenda. Careful preparation is essential to make presentations that involve your listeners. A speaker must also know how to use energy to deliver ideas with maximum impact. Finally, speaking and listening skills help create a consensus. Effective communication skills—writing, speaking, and listening—can build an atmosphere of cooperation between employees and make every meeting far more productive.

EXERCISE

Evaluate the next meeting you attend and answer the following questions.

1. Did the meeting have a clearly written agenda that was circulated to participants in advance?

2. Did the meeting leader keep the discussion focused on the agenda items?

3. Did the meeting leader give everyone an opportunity to participate?

4. Were the presentations at the meeting well prepared? *(Continued on page 124)*

(Continued from page 123)

5. Did presenters make their purpose clear and speak with energy?

6. Did all the participants use active listening skills?

7. Was a consensus reached by the end of the meeting?

8. Were there specific action steps?

GLOSSARY

Agenda. A careful structure for a meeting that explains what is to be covered during it.

Application letter. A letter briefly describing your qualifications for a job.

Cross-functional team. A group of employees from different departments of a company brought together to solve a problem or accomplish a task as a team.

E-mail. Electronic mail sent via computer and telephone lines from one person to another.

Listener analysis. An evaluation of your audience which helps you in preparing a talk.

Milestones. Checkpoints during the process of completing a project intended to insure that the final deadline will be met.

Pyramid style. An approach to writing in which the most important information is placed at the beginning.

Resume. A brief listing of your job objective, education, and job experience that is used to apply for employment.

Stage fright. Fear of speaking in front of an audience.

Summary sentences. The sentences that summarize the purpose of a piece of writing.

3Ts. An effective method of organizing a presentation by introducing a subject, describing its key elements, and then briefly repeating them at the conclusion.

BIBLIOGRAPHY

Angell, David and Brent Heslop. *The Elements of E-Mail Style.* Reading, MA: Addison Wesley, 1994.

Anderson, Richard. *Writing That Works.* New York: McGraw-Hill, 1987.

Chang, Richard and Kevin Kehoe. *Meetings That Work.* Irvine, CA: Chang Associates, 1994.

Jeary, Tony. *Inspire Any Audience.* Dallas: Trophy Publishing, 1996.

Kops, George and Richard Worth. *Great Speaches Aren't Born.* Hollywood, FL.: Lifetime Books, 1996.

Mosvick, Roger and Robert Nelson. *We've Got To Start Meeting Like This.* Indianapolis: Park Avenue Productions, 1996.

Paolo, Frank. *How To Make a Great Presentation in 2 Hours.* Hollywood, FL: Lifetime Books, 1993.

Plotnik, Arthur. *The Elements of Expression.* New York: Henry Holt, 1996.

Richardson, Bradley. *Jobsmarts for Twentysomethings.* New York: Random House, 1995.

Roman, Kenneth and Joel Raphaelson. *Writing That Works.* New York: HarperCollins, 1992.

Sant, Tom. *Pursuasive Business Proposals.* New York: Amacom, 1992.

Simmons, Curt. *Public Speaking Made Simple.* New York, Main Street Books, 1996.

Walton, Donald. *Are You Communicating?* New York: McGraw-Hill, 1989.